THE LIBRARY OF WEAPONS OF MASS DESTRUCTION™

America's Star Wars Program

ANN BYERS

The Rosen Publishing Group, Inc., New York

To my father, Joseph Garrity, an American patriot

Published in 2005 by The Rosen Publishing Group, Inc.
29 East 21st Street, New York, NY 10010

First Edition

Library of Congress Cataloging-in-Publication Data

Byers, Ann.
America's Star Wars program / by Ann Byers.
    p. cm. — (The library of weapons of mass destruction)
Includes bibliographical references and index.
ISBN 1-4042-0287-0 (library binding)
1. Ballistic missile defenses—United States—Juvenile literature.
I. Title. II. Series.
UG743.B94 2005
358.1'74'0973—dc22

2004014803

Manufactured in the United States of America

On the cover: Computer artwork depicts two military satellites firing lasers at unidentified targets as part of Strategic Defense Initiative.

[CONTENTS]

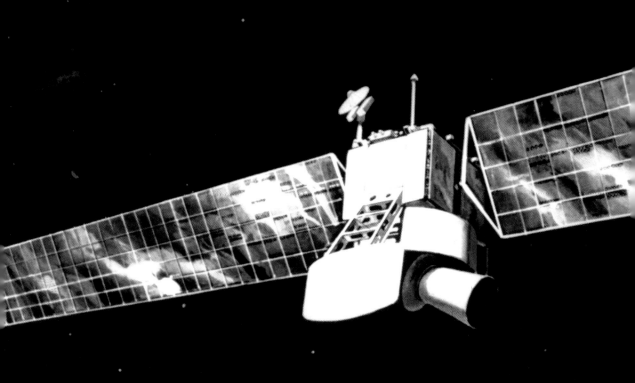

INTRODUCTION

The attack came without warning. In a lightning flash, the first rocket streaked skyward. Within seconds, others followed. After years of waiting, the evil empire had finally struck. But, although the barrage was sudden, the soldiers were ready. The shield shot up and they manned their stations. From the battleships in space, weapons were fired: lasers, ray guns, and blasters. The bullets homed in on the enemy rockets and blasted them to pieces. The defenses worked; the enemy attack failed.

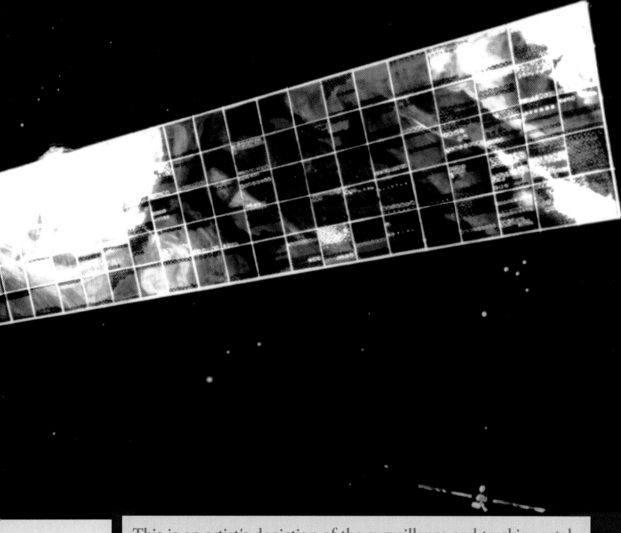

This is an artist's depiction of the surveillance and tracking satellite that was to be part of the U.S. government's Strategic Defense Initiative. Ideally, a network of satellites such as this would detect and track all objects that may be orbiting Earth, discriminating against ballistic missiles, decoys, and debris.

Does this sound like a scene from George Lucas's fictional *Star Wars*? It is actually a scenario from a very serious, nonfictional Star Wars. This Star Wars was one of a number of programs that was developed to defend the United States against a possible military attack.

For nearly 200 years, the United States felt protected from outside attacks by its miles of shoreline. Two vast oceans separate the American continent from most potential enemies. However, that feeling of security eroded with the advent of the missile age following World War II

(1939–1945). For the first time in history, it appeared that weapons launched overseas could reach American cities in hours. From the 1950s on, the U.S. government has had the responsibility of protecting its citizens from threats of missile attacks from other nations.

Over the decades, the nature of the threats has changed. Different countries have posed new dangers. Innovative weapons have created additional challenges. But the need for defense has remained. This book explores ways the United States has attempted to shield itself from foreign missile attacks. ■

An intercontinental ballistic missile is pictured here within its silo. Missile silos, built underground, are meant to provide protection for the missile against an enemy attack. However, as the accuracy of guidance systems has improved over the years, silos can only provide so much protection. Today, most of the United States' ICBMs are placed on submarines.

MISSILE WARS

A missile is an object that is thrown or propelled. Rocks, spears, arrows, and bullets can all be missiles. A missile used as a modern weapon has three parts: a power source, a guidance system, and a payload. The power source is what starts the missile toward its target. The guidance system keeps it moving in the right direction. The payload is the object the missile carries—the whole reason for having and using the missile. When a missile is used as a weapon, the payload is a warhead. The warhead is the explosive part, or the part that does the damage.

Because they have guidance or control systems, these modern weapons are called guided missiles. Two types of guided missiles are used in warfare today: cruise missiles and ballistic missiles. Cruise missiles are aerodynamic. That is, their paths are affected by the air through which they travel. The paths of ballistic missiles are affected not by air, but by how they are projected or fired.

Cruise missiles are basically small airplanes without pilots. The power source that launches them is a turbojet or turbofan engine. The engine continues to power them until they reach their target. They can be guided in flight by remote control, a radio signal, a target-seeking radar (such as a heat sensor), or other navigation devices. After they are launched, flip-out wings open, providing stability and making them easy to maneuver.

Cruise missiles fly much like airplanes. They operate in Earth's atmosphere, usually no higher than about 50 feet (15 meters). They travel at about the same speed as airplanes, up to 550 miles per hour (885 kilometers per hour). Except for guidance adjustments, they move in straight lines. Cruise missiles can cover distances of 65 miles (105 km) to 1,860 miles (3,000 km). These distances are considered short-range. The payloads of short-range missiles are usually high-explosive warheads. However, because cruise missiles are more stable than their ballistic cousins, they are suitable for carrying chemical or biological warheads.

A ballistic missile is much bigger and faster than a cruise missile. It is sleek, without wings or fins. Its power source is a rocket. The rocket only gets the missile started. After the rocket's fuel burns off, the missile operates without any power and continues on the path on which it was launched. Some ballistic missiles have more than one rocket, firing in stages. At each stage, the rocket can be fired in a way that changes the missile's course slightly.

Unlike a cruise missile that travels low and in a straight line, a ballistic missile rises in an arc high above Earth. It has three phases. The

The Tomahawk cruise missile can hit targets on land and at sea. It has the ability to fly at low altitudes and, thus, avoid being detected. It is computer-guided, making it able to reach targets with great accuracy. This cruise missile's first operational use was by the United States during the Gulf War in Iraq in 1991.

boost phase is the powered portion of the flight. The rocket, or rockets, thrust the missile above or to the edge of Earth's atmosphere. This takes no more than five minutes. In the midcourse phase, the rockets, which are no longer needed, drop off, leaving only the warhead. The warhead's path is set, and it coasts along that path, usually outside Earth's atmosphere, for as long as twenty minutes. When the warhead reenters the atmosphere, the terminal phase begins. The terminal phase can be as brief as thirty seconds, and the warhead can be traveling as quickly as 2,000 miles (3,219 km) per hour.

Ballistic missiles can be short-, medium-, or long-range. Short- and medium-range ballistic missiles are theater missiles, which means they are used in theaters, or areas, of war. They usually have high-explosive warheads. They can also carry chemical or biological warheads. Long-range missiles are often strategic weapons, used to carry out a nation's strategy of hitting its target at its military, economic, or political source. They do not carry chemical or biological weapons. The chemicals or organisms would likely be destroyed by the intense heat of reentry. Longer-range missiles often carry nuclear payloads. The most powerful long-range weapon, an intercontinental ballistic missile (ICBM), can sail 6,200 miles (10,000 km) across the ocean in half an hour. Larger ICBMs can carry more than one warhead.

Missiles can be classified according to their launch and target sites. For example, an air-to-surface missile is launched from a plane in the air at a target on the surface of the land or water. Cruise missiles are either air-to-surface or surface-to-surface. Ballistic missiles can be surface-to-surface or surface-to-air.

MISSILE DEFENSE

Antiaircraft guns and fighter planes were used during the first attempts to defend against modern missiles. Toward the end of World War II, Nazi Germany surprised Europe with two new types of weapons. The V-1, called a buzz bomb, was basically a cruise missile. It was used to inflict terror and damage on Allied cities. The V-2 rocket bomb was the first ballistic missile.

American and British forces, part of the Allied forces, shot down many of the V-1s while they were in the air. The V-2s, however, were much too fast for the Allied planes and guns. The Allies tried to find the rockets' launchers and destroy them before they could get the weapons in the air. But the launchers were well hidden and none were destroyed.

After the war, both the United States and the Soviet Union began developing ballistic missiles. Both countries employed some of the German scientists who had created the V-2s. The United States was suspicious of the Soviets. They were Communist, and they were trying to make many other countries Communist. U.S. officials were afraid the Soviet Union might attack the United States. They worried that the Soviets would build a weapon that could reach America and that the weapon could carry an atomic warhead. American armed forces wanted to work on an antiballistic missile—an antimissile missile.

But most scientists said it could not be done, at least with the technology they had then. The U.S. president, General Dwight D. Eisenhower (1890–1969), dismissed the idea of "hitting a bullet with a bullet." However, in 1957, two events changed the minds of many leaders. The first occurred in August, when the Soviet Union tested an ICBM. This weapon had the ability to hit and destroy U.S. fleets and perhaps American cities. Worries that the Soviets might develop a weapon that could reach the United States had become a reality.

In October of the same year, the Soviets stunned the world by placing *Sputnik I*, the first artificial satellite, in orbit. U.S. scientists feared that the Soviets might be able to launch missiles from the satellite. American citizens were terrified with *Sputnik I* flying directly above the United States. The need for defense against Soviet missiles seemed urgent.

NIKE-ZEUS

The army began research on an antimissile program in 1958. It already had Nikes—surface-to-air antiaircraft missiles. It would adapt the Nike to become an antiballistic missile (ABM), shooting down warheads instead of airplanes. It dubbed the new weapon "Zeus." The army's plan was to build dish-type radar that could detect incoming missiles and pinpoint their paths. The Zeus, armed with a 400-kiloton nuclear warhead, would intercept the missile in its midcourse phase, at least sixty miles (97 km) above Earth.

Scientists saw many problems with the Nike-Zeus program. The radar system was questioned. It did not appear sophisticated enough to identify and track such fast-moving weapons that would be launched without warning. Besides, the Soviets could send up several ICBMs at once. They could also launch decoys along with the active warheads to confuse the radar. Some scientists worried that when the ABM's warhead exploded, nuclear fallout could disable the radar. The program did not have a strong enough chance of success to justify its expense. The research was done, but no system was built. In 1961 President John F. Kennedy (1917–1963) disbanded the program.

The V-2 rocket *(bottom right)* was the world's first ballistic missile. Germany built 10,000 of these unmanned, guided "robot bombers." The V-2 ultimately failed as a weapon due to its small warhead and inaccuracy, but 1,000 of these missiles were fired on London and other cities in Great Britain, causing such damage as seen here in London. An additional 3,000 hit other targeted cities in Europe. After V-2 rockets were introduced, the Allies began their own efforts to duplicate and improve upon them.

A Nike-Zeus missile is pictured here on its launchpad at White Sands, New Mexico. It was first tested in August 1959 and reached a top speed of 8,000 miles (12,875 km) per hour. Nike-Zeus—an improved-upon version of the Nike-Hercules—was meant to intercept ballistic missile reentry vehicles. It was the largest single-chamber, solid-fuel booster produced in the United States at the time, providing 450,000 pounds (204,116 kg) of thrust.

PROJECT DEFENDER

At the same time that the army was working on Nike-Zeus, the Pentagon's research arm was exploring other defense options. This research was called Project Defender. One outcome of these studies was the Ballistic Missile Boost Intercept (BAMBI) program. BAMBI was a space-based program designed to intercept enemy missiles in the boost phase. Launchers were to be placed in satellites orbiting directly over the Soviet Union. The warheads would not be nuclear, but would deploy wire meshes that could disable ICBMs as they were just getting off the ground.

Like Nike-Zeus, Project Defender was too costly and did not seem practical. Even if the interceptors could perform as planned, the satellites were vulnerable to attack. The project was canceled in 1968.

THE MINUTEMAN MISSILE

Minuteman is an intercontinental ballistic missile. The first Minuteman was ready for operation in 1962. Powered by three solid-fueled rocket engines, it can travel at 15,000 miles (24,140 km) per hour and cover more than 8,000 miles (12,875 km). Each Minuteman carries multiple nuclear warheads, able to strike different targets. The most advanced missile, Minuteman III, costs $1,818,000.

Each Minuteman is kept on alert in an underground tube 80 feet (24.4 m) deep, covered by a 100-ton door. To launch the missile, the door must be blasted open. Groups of ten missiles are arranged in circles around launch control centers. The missiles are at least 3 miles (5 km) apart, and the groups at least 14 miles (22.5 km) apart. The launch control center, which is manned around the clock, is buried like the missiles—40 to 100 feet (12 to 30.5 m) below ground. In order for the missile to be fired, at least two launch control centers have to give the launch command.

A Minuteman III missile, pictured here in its silo, was an improvement on the Minuteman I and II. The Minuteman III had an increased payload and was touted to survive a nuclear environment. There are 500 Minuteman III missiles at four bases in the north-central part of the United States. From the beginning, the Minuteman program was a quick-reacting and highly survivable addition to the United States' nuclear arsenal.

NIKE-X

The army still thought its Nike missiles could be used. In 1963 it redesigned its missile defense strategy, calling the new system Nike-X. Nike-X used two different types of ABMs. The Spartan was a long-range Zeus missile that would intercept an incoming weapon in mid-course. In case the Spartan failed, a short-range Sprint would shoot down the enemy missile in its terminal phase. This is called a layered defense: one missile for above-earth interception and another one for the lower-altitude layer.

The Nike-X program used a new and better radar and upgraded control systems. It looked like it might work. But before any Nike-X system could be put in place, U.S. politicians changed the defense plan. ■

2

NATIONAL SHIELD

From 1945 to 1990, the United States and the Soviet Union were engaged in an intense conflict. The two countries had drastically different political, economic, and social systems. Both had become very powerful, and neither trusted the other. To the United States, it looked like the Communist Soviet Union was trying to turn every nation it could into a Communist country it could control. Indeed, the Soviet Union was interested in security and protection for itself against any foes: the country had been attacked twice in the first half of the twentieth century, causing 25 to 50 million

A convoy of military trucks parades its interceptor missiles, dubbed the Galosh missiles by the United States, in front of the Lenin Memorial at Red Square in Moscow as part of the May Day festivities in 1964. Soviet technologists made up for this missile's inaccuracy by arming it with a nuclear weapon that yielded roughly one megaton—an amount that would kill within a radius of 19 miles (31 km).

deaths. The whole world had witnessed the United States drop the atom bomb on two cities in Japan, effectively ending World War II. The Soviet Union feared that it could be a target of the United States.

Suspicion and disagreements between the superpowers were great, but they stopped short of direct military combat. Because of this, the conflict was dubbed the Cold War. For the entire period, and especially in the earlier years, politicians worried that the cold, or nonfighting, war could become hot.

These fears led to an arms race. Both countries sped to build the biggest and best arsenal before the other. At first, in the 1960s, it looked like the Soviets might be winning. In 1961, they fired a fifty-eight-megaton nuclear bomb with more explosive power than all the bombs

U.S. president Richard Nixon *(left)* and general secretary Leonid Brezhnev *(right)* conclude two and a half years of negotiations that were SALT I, with the signing of the ABM Treaty, the SALT Accord, and the Interim Agreement on the Limitation of Strategic Offensive Arms on May 26, 1972, in Moscow. SALT I limited each superpower's ballistic missile defense, as well as halted its ballistic missile launchers.

WORLD DIVISION...
.....COLD WAR ARITHMETIC

GREENLAND

CANADA

NORTH AMERICA

U.S.A.

WASHINGTON

CUBA
?

ATLANTIC OCEAN

PACIFIC OCEAN

SOUTH AMERICA

ENGLAND

FRANCE

EUROPE

MOSCOW

TURKEY

CAIRO

U.A.

AFRICA

—LEGEND—

///// ALIGNED WITH WEST

PRO-RED BLOC

NEUTRAL

POPULATION

990 MILLION

1,025 MILLION

875 MILLION

U.S.S.R.

ASIA

PEIPING

CHINA

JAPAN

INDIA

PACIFIC

OCEAN

PHILIPPINES

INDONES

NDIAN

OCEAN

A

This map, dated July 16, 1960, depicts the standings of each nation in their leanings during the early period of the Cold War. Due to their large populations, those nations that claimed to be neutral were areas of intense focus of the United States and the Soviet Union. Cuba has a question mark because, at this date, it was part of the Rio Pact, a nonaggression treaty between the United States and nineteen Latin American countries, signed in 1947. However, even then, Cuba was already showing its strong "red" leanings.

A Minuteman III missile is being returned to its underground silo by a transporter-erector vehicle in Peetz, Colorado, after undergoing guidance system upgrades. The Minuteman ICBMs were designed to be launched on short notice. The first Minuteman went on alert during the Cuban missile crisis. The Minuteman III was deployed in 1970.

used in World War II. In 1962, the Soviets positioned nuclear missiles close to the United States, on the island of Cuba. In 1964, they started construction of an antimissile system to protect their capital, Moscow, in Russia. They put a large number of ABMs on public display in that city.

Meanwhile, during the time of the Cold War, the United States stationed nuclear weapons in twenty-seven countries around the world, including Iceland, Germany, Japan, and along the Soviet border of Turkey. Although the United States consistently and publicly denied this in the case of Turkey, the Soviet Union was well aware of this arsenal.

Still, people worried that the Soviet Union could mount a surprise attack and the United States could not defend itself. They began to talk of a "missile gap," wondering if the Soviet Union was far ahead of the United States in missile technology.

Although it appeared that the Soviets might be ahead, the United States always had the edge. America's missiles were far better. The Soviets had more ballistic missiles, but it has since been revealed they did not have the warheads for them. Still, at the time, U.S. Secretary of Defense Robert McNamara (1916–) was alarmed. He thought that if the Soviets did attack, even with poorer quality weapons, they could inflict serious damage. The United States could not build enough ABM systems to stop the number of missiles the Soviets could launch. McNamara felt that the only way to avoid nuclear war was to persuade the Soviet Union not to strike—to deter the Soviets from using their weapons. He reasoned that if either the United States or the Soviet Union attacked, the other country would surely fight back and both could be destroyed.

He called this scenario "assured destruction." He assured the Soviet Union that if it were to send a missile to the United States, the United States would unleash enough of its missiles to wipe out 20 to 25 percent of the Soviet Union's population and 50 percent of its industrial ability. Thus, McNamara shifted the nation's defense strategy from protection to deterrence. If deterrence worked, he explained, defensive weapons would not be necessary. He then concentrated on building up the offensive arsenal. He deployed fifty-four Titan II and 1,000 Minuteman missiles on land and 656 Polaris missiles on forty-one nuclear submarines.

ROBERT MCNAMARA, IN A SEPTEMBER 18, 1967, SPEECH TO THE AMERICAN PUBLIC

"Is the Soviet Union seriously attempting to acquire a first-strike capability against the United States? Although this is a question we cannot answer with absolute certainty, we believe the answer is no. In any event, the question itself is—in a sense—irrelevant: for the United States will maintain and, where necessary strengthen its retaliatory forces so that, whatever the Soviet Union's intentions or actions, we will continue to have an assured-destruction capability . . ."

President Lyndon B. Johnson *(far left)* and Secretary of Defense Robert McNamara *(second from left)* attend a National Security Council meeting on February 7, 1968. McNamara resigned shortly afterward and became head of the World Bank. Before accepting President Kennedy's invitation to serve as secretary of defense in 1960, McNamara had worked for Ford Motor Company, becoming the first president of the company outside of Henry Ford's family.

SENTINEL

Meanwhile, a new threat emerged. By 1967, the People's Republic of China, another Communist country, had atomic bombs, hydrogen bombs, and nuclear ballistic missiles. Analysts feared it could have an ICBM within a few years. McNamara thought the policy of deterrence would work with the Soviet Union, but no one knew what China might do. China did not have many nuclear weapons. Unlike the Soviet Union, which could stage a massive assault, China was capable of only a limited attack. But even a limited attack could be deadly. Some defense against a small-scale strike was necessary.

In September 1967, McNamara announced that the United States would develop a "thin shield," an umbrella of ABMs covering major cities that would protect them from a limited attack. This missile shield was called Sentinel. It made use of the Nike-X technology, a layered defense using Spartan and Sprint missiles. It called for 700 ABMs.

The idea of a missile defense shield was controversial. Scientists and politicians argued for and against Sentinel. Opponents claimed that defensive antimissiles were less effective and more expensive than offensive weapons. Proponents countered that defense systems were needed to protect the offensive weapons in the event of a strike. Those opposed believed that developing new weapons, even defensive ones, would intensify the arms race. Those in favor believed that a good defense could end the arms race. Some people said that a limited shield was useless because one missile that got through would cause terrible damage. Others pointed out that saving a few people would be better than saving none.

McNamara himself did not really support the program. He thought deterrence was better than defense. He proposed it as a compromise— a limited system that probably would not anger the Soviet Union but would make some Americans feel safer.

When it was time to actually implement the program, the general public began to protest. Citizens who lived near the proposed missile sites were concerned that their cities could become targets for Soviet ICBMs. They worried that the ABMs might accidentally detonate. Many people wanted protection from nuclear weapons, but they did not want that protection in their backyards.

SAFEGUARD

When Richard Nixon became president in 1969, he tried to calm public fears. He decided not to place the ABMs near cities. Instead, he would position them close to the country's offensive missiles. The offensive ballistic missiles were housed in silos in remote areas. The new plan, called Safeguard, would shield missiles rather than people.

The move was not enough to stop criticism. When Congress voted on whether to give funds to build the Safeguard system, the measure passed by only one vote. It took six years and $5 billion to build just one Safeguard site.

At the time Congress was debating the value of the Safeguard missile shield, the president was trying to persuade the Soviets to sit down and discuss the problem of weapons proliferation. Nixon knew that there

was only one way that the United States could protect itself from a Soviet attack: to deter the Soviet Union by letting it know that regardless of who struck first, the retaliation would be so devastating that both countries would be destroyed. Nixon's revamping of McNamara's "assured destruction" policy became known as mutual assured destruction, or MAD. Nixon knew that the only way deterrence would work was if the Soviets also understood the repercussions of attacking. Nixon finally succeeded in arranging a series of meetings with Soviet leader Leonid Brezhnev (1906–1982), called Strategic Arms Limitation Talks, or SALT.

SALT

The purpose of the meetings, as the name suggests, was to reach agreement on limiting strategic arms. Strategic arms are any weapons, offensive or defensive, used to carry

The U.S. Army's White Sands Missile Range is located 30 miles (48 km) from Alamogordo, New Mexico, where the first nuclear weapon was detonated, known as the Trinity Test. Above is the antimissile system complex, where transmitter radar tops the building to the left, and the radome, to the right, houses receiving antennae.

out a nation's strategy, or general plan. The strategic arms the United States was concerned with were ballistic missiles and antiballistic missiles.

Distrust was so strong between the two governments that it took five years of negotiations (from 1964 to 1969) just for their leaders to agree to the talks. Then the first round of SALT meetings took more than two years, from November 1969 to January 1972, to reach any agreement. Throughout the process, the arms race continued. Both sides kept trying to develop new and better weapons. Although the goal of the talks was equality, neither country wanted to be lagging behind the other.

When agreements were finally reached, they were historic. The two documents signed on May 26, 1972, by President Richard Nixon of the United States and Communist Party general secretary Leonid Brezhnev of the Soviet Union, put the brakes on the arms buildup. One was the Interim Agreement on the Limitation of Strategic Offensive Arms, known as the SALT I Treaty. The other was the Anti-Ballistic Missile Treaty, or the ABM Treaty.

The SALT I Treaty froze the number of offensive weapons each country had. Neither could build any new missile launchers. They could not make any new kinds of missiles. But they could make the missiles they had better. The treaty listed the numbers each country had, and they agreed to keep to those numbers. SALT I was an interim agreement, binding for only five years.

THE ABM TREATY

The other agreement that emerged from the SALT meetings limited defensive weapons. The purpose of the ABM Treaty was to make sure that the two countries would not have or develop national defense systems. The reasoning was that if neither nation had a defense shield, the MAD fear would keep each from attacking the other. If one country felt safe under some kind of umbrella, it would have no deterrence restraining it from launching an assault. Instead of a national defense system that would protect the entire country, each country could have two small systems that guarded two small sites. In 1974, the treaty was

Richard Nixon and Leonid Brezhnev exchange signed copies of the SALT I Treaty on May 26, 1972, while Soviet and U.S. officials look on. The treaty held each party accountable to the measures negotiated in halting the arms race. The treaty emphasized reductions that could be measured from afar, including destroying silos and submarines.

amended so that each party was reduced to one defensive system at one location.

The treaty defined an ABM system as a set of devices used to defend against strategic ballistic missiles while they are in flight. ABM systems, according to the treaty, consist of missile launchers, interceptors (the missiles), and radars. Each of these parts was severely restricted by the treaty. The number of missiles was limited: no more than 100 for each country. And no missile could have more than one warhead (even though ballistic missiles could have multiple warheads). The kind of launcher was specified: each launcher could fire only one missile at a time, and no rapid-reload launchers were permitted. The systems had to be land-based; they could not be on ships, submarines, or satellites. They had to be fixed; they could not be able to be moved from one location to another.

Unlike the SALT I agreement, the ABM Treaty had no expiration date. It was to be reviewed every five years. If either party wanted to withdraw, it had to give six months' notice.

The Soviet Union chose to use its one allowable ABM system to defend its capital, Moscow. The United States decided to use the Safeguard program it had been building as its ABM system. It was at the Grand Forks Air Base near Fargo, North Dakota. The U.S. system would protect the Minuteman ballistic missiles that were deployed there. The site was finally completed and began operation on October 1, 1975. The very next day Congress voted to withdraw funding for Safeguard. Congressmen reasoned that the few ABMs deployed in North Dakota would be no match for the large number of ballistic missiles the Soviets had. After only four months of operation, Safeguard was shut down. So after February 1976, America had no missile defense.

In negotiating the ABM Treaty, the diplomats discussed what might happen if one country developed an entirely new kind of defense system. What if weapons were created that did not use the kind of launchers, interceptors, or radars so carefully defined in the treaty? Scientists were working on ideas that seemed quite far-fetched at the time: lasers, particle beams, and other futuristic devices. Some of the negotiators wanted to ban nearly everything. Others wanted to let scientists keep researching new things. In the end, they decided that scientists could explore the possibilities of defensive weapons that did not violate treaty principles. If and when they actually invented any weapons, a committee would figure out what to do about them at that time.

This was the only loophole in the treaty that allowed work on missile defense to continue. Six years after the treaty was signed, president Ronald Reagan (1911–2004) was to take advantage of this loophole. ■

Ronald Reagan speaks to the American public on March 23, 1983. It was during this speech that he outlined the Strategic Defense Initiative that would be dubbed Star Wars. The Soviet Union saw the program as a threat to its security, as the United States would be able to launch an attack without any fear of retaliation from the Soviet Union.

STAR WARS

When Ronald Reagan became president in 1981, the Cold War climate was still very icy. The Soviet Union had openly declared that its goal was to communize the world. It had crushed rebellions in Czechoslovakia and invaded Afghanistan. Cuba had fallen to Communism. The Soviet Union was supporting revolutions in Latin America. Reagan and most other U.S. citizens believed that if it could, the Soviet Union would not hesitate to try to extend its rule over the United States. Both the United States and the Soviet Union thought that the other might be cheating on the SALT agreements, secretly working on new weapons.

Reagan did not agree with the MAD logic of mutual assured destruction. He believed that the United States needed to be stronger than the Soviet Union. He criticized the way previous presidents had failed to build up American armed forces. In the nine years since SALT I, the United States had built almost no new weapons at all. Soldiers and sailors were being trained with old equipment, completely unprepared for any attack. At the same time, the Soviets were deploying a new missile with three warheads every week, despite the terms of any treaty. During his campaign Reagan warned, "This nation has become number two in a world where it is dangerous—if not fatal—to be second best."

Reagan wanted peace, but he believed the only way to achieve that peace was through strength. "If you were going to approach the Russians with a dove of peace in one hand," he said, "you had to have a sword in the other." Building up the military was Reagan's top priority. SALT I forbade developing new types of ICBMs, but it did not prohibit improving the ones the country already had. Nor did it limit construction of conventional weapons—planes, bombs, and short-range missiles. Under Reagan, Congress spent billions of dollars on the biggest peacetime military expansion in the nation's history. One hundred B-1 bombers were made to replace the older B-52s. Intercontinental-range missiles were modernized with 100 new weapons, the MX Peacekeepers. Nuclear submarines were updated. Work began on a Stealth bomber and on satellites for military communication.

ARMS REDUCTION AND DEFENSE

Now Reagan felt he could talk with the Soviets from a position of strength. He wanted to go beyond the SALT meetings. SALT had to do with arms limitation; Reagan wanted arms reduction. He changed SALT—strategic arms limitation talks—to START—Strategic Arms Reduction Talks. His real dream was even beyond START—more than nuclear arms reduction, he wanted nuclear weapons elimination. As far as he was concerned, "the MAD policy [on which SALT was based] was madness."

But the Soviet Union did not want to seriously reduce, much less do away with, its nuclear arsenal. Many of Reagan's advisers felt that the United States needed to maintain its nuclear capability also. The president knew that he could not rid the world of nuclear weapons. But, he said, "I had this second dream: the creation of a defense against nuclear missiles, so we could change from a policy of assured destruction to one of assured survival."

Reagan's dream of a strong national defense was challenged before he was even elected president. In 1979, he visited the North American Aerospace Defense (NORAD) center in Cheyenne Mountain in Colorado. This is the facility that would warn of any air attack coming upon the United States. A tour of the center includes a simulation, or pretend display, of NORAD's systems. Reagan watched as a red light on a map showed the beginning of a mock attack. It indicated that a missile had been fired from North Korea toward the United States. (This was, of course, a completely hypothetical drill. The United States knew that North Korea did not have this capability at the time.) It took a minute for NORAD's radars to pick up the mock missile. The system reported the time and place of the launch. It took a few more seconds before the missile actually showed up on the radar screen. By that time, it was nearly to its destination in Alaska. With everyone else, Reagan waited for a U.S. ABM to destroy the deadly weapon. But the interception did not come. In 1979, the United States had a great early-warning system, but it had no defense system capable of acting on the warning.

THE IDEA

Reagan may have been frustrated by his nation's powerlessness against attack, but he was not defeated. He had an idea for a new kind of defense. The concept had begun to take shape thirteen years earlier, during another tour. In 1967, Reagan, then newly elected governor of California, had visited the Lawrence Livermore National Laboratory near San Francisco.

One of the directors of the weapons laboratory, Edward Teller (1908–2003), was firmly convinced that a national defense system was not only possible, but absolutely necessary. He believed that the

NORAD/USSPACECOM
COMMAND CENTER

COMMAND AUTHORITIES

UNITED STATES
PRES WASHINGTON DC
VICE ENRT ANDREWS AFB
SECDEF WASHINGTON DC
CJCS WASHINGTON DC

CANADA
PM OTTAWA
MND OTTAWA
CDS OTTAWA
VCDS MACEDONIA

US Element NORAD

PRI VADM BROWNE
SEC BRIG GEN LATIFF

DELTA Crew

CD	MGEN	BARTRAM
MD	COL	BRILLS
MO	LT COL	COX
AO	CAPT	WELCH
EA	RMC	MCENTARF
EA	SRA	HUTCHINS
EA		

ASSESSORS

NORAD
PRI VADM BROWNE
SEC MGEN BARTRAM

USSPACECOM
PRI VADM BROWNE
SEC BRIG GEN LATIFF

20:14:31   14:14:31   10:14:31   13:14:

ZULU   EXERCISE   HAWAII   PACIFIC

34

EXER

Soviets had the beginnings of such a system. He also thought they were secretly making offensive weapons that were far better than those of the United States. Teller had been designing some very different types of weapons. He could work on these weapons without violating the ABM Treaty because they were not ballistic.

Teller's plan was to shoot down enemy missiles not with ballistic weapons, but with lasers. A ballistic weapon is a projected missile that carries a warhead. It can be thought of like an arrow: launching the shaft delivers the arrowhead, which inflicts the damage. A laser is a device that sends out high energy, which can be deadly because it is concentrated. It is a little like a powerful fire hose: the force of the water can knock a person over. Teller was sure he could build lasers so

The North American Aerospace Defense, commonly referred to as NORAD, is located deep inside Cheyenne Mountain in Colorado. The motto of this military command station is to deter, detect, and defend. Here, a screen displays the where-abouts of U.S. and Canadian political leaders. Before the terrorist attacks on September 11, 2001, NORAD mostly focused on threats that could come far away from U.S. and Canadian borders, but since then, the focus has shifted to controlling airspace over the two nations.

Dr. Edward Teller is pictured here in his office at Stanford University in 1986. Known for championing the development of the hydrogen bomb and the Strategic Defense Initiative, he is considered one of the most influential scientists of the Cold War, influencing presidents from both parties. He once stated, "The second half of the century has been incomparably more peaceful than the first, simply by putting power into the hands of those people who wanted peace."

powerful their beams could disable any ICBM.

In 1967, Reagan listened to Teller for two hours. He asked questions. He seemed intrigued. But he was only governor of a state, and he had little power over what the national government might do. And in 1967, the popular stance was the MAD position: the best defense was no defense at all.

THE STRATEGIC DEFENSE INITIATIVE

When Reagan became president fourteen years later, Teller contacted him again. Teller's lab had constructed and tested an X-ray laser. It worked perfectly. It was still only a test model, but the successful test showed that the idea was sound. Teller envisioned his lasers on satellites orbiting Earth.

They would provide a blanket of protection not only for the United States, but for all of its allies as well. But Reagan did not seem interested.

The president was still trying to convince the Soviet Union that both countries should begin to destroy their nuclear weapons. He even wrote a personal letter to Leonid Brezhnev, who had signed the SALT treaties. But the Soviets refused. Publicly and privately, Reagan accused Brezhnev of building weapons in violation of their agreements. As he bolstered America's offensive strength, he wanted to build up defenses, too. But no one had an idea how to do that without going against the ABM Treaty—no one except Edward Teller and a handful of scientists.

Dr. Teller received a phone call inviting him to a dinner at the White House in March 1983. He had no idea why the president wanted to meet with him. In fact, almost no one had any clue that Reagan was about to radically alter America's Cold War policy. He was scheduled to make a speech that was to be televised, but it was nothing big. It was merely a routine explanation of his budget for the military. But he had inserted something new in his speech. His top advisers learned of the change only a few hours before the broadcast.

The opening lines of the March 23 address hinted at something major. "I've reached a decision," he told the American people. He said that the "strategy of deterrence . . . still works, but what it takes to maintain deterrence has changed." The new world, ten years after the SALT meetings and the ABM Treaty, required different kinds of weapons. It required strong defense as well as a good offense. The president used photographs to illustrate the seriousness of the Soviet threat. He reminded his audience that every item, every expenditure, for defense was "intended for one all-important purpose: to keep the peace."

Then came the bomb—Reagan's "vision of the future which offers hope." First he spoke directly to Teller and the others who had just eaten dinner with him: "I call upon the scientific community . . . to give us the means of rendering . . . nuclear weapons impotent and obsolete." He was inviting the scientists to come up with a missile shield that would make it useless for any nation to try to attack the United States with nuclear weapons. Developing that shield would take time and money. So he

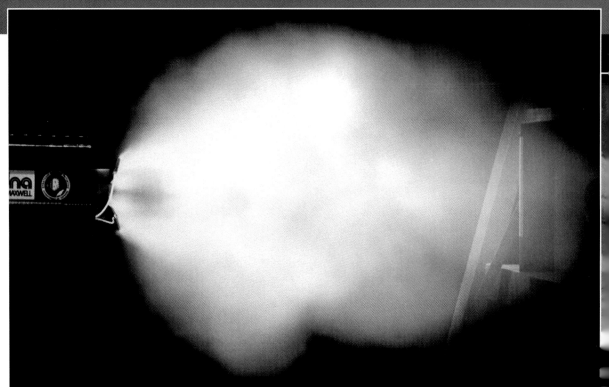

38

Pictured here are various examples of research that were part of the Star Wars program. A railgun *(top left)* fires a projectile through a steel plate, using electromagnetism as a propellant. A Titan I missile *(center)* is destroyed with a chemical laser, taking several seconds to destroy the liquid-propelled ballistic missile. Above, the red glow of a neutral particle beam accelerator burns a hole into aluminum. At left, this time-lapsed photo shows a low-powered laser tracking a rocket as part of a test to verify viability of ground-based lasers against an enemy's ballistic missile in space.

announced: "I am directing a comprehensive and intensive effort to define a long-term research and development program to begin to achieve our ultimate goal of eliminating the threat posed by strategic nuclear missiles." He was giving the scientists the funds they would need. He called his proposal the Strategic Defense Initiative, or SDI.

THE REACTION

Even Reagan's advisers were stunned. Without consulting them, without much study, and without public debate, he had launched a program that would change the way the two superpowers related to each other. America's allies were equally surprised. They worried that if the United States sheltered itself behind a missile shield, the Soviet Union might turn its weapons on them.

The U.S. Congress was divided. Just an hour after Reagan's announcement of the initiative, Senator Ted Kennedy (1932–) criticized it, calling it "Star Wars" after the popular science-fiction movie. He and

RONALD REAGAN ANNOUNCES THE STRATEGIC DEFENSE INITIATIVE

"The United States does not start fights. We will never be an aggressor. We maintain our strength in order to preserve freedom and peace . . . What if free people could live secure in the knowledge that we could intercept and destroy strategic ballistic missiles before they reached our own soil or that of our allies? . . . We seek neither military superiority nor political advantage. Our only purpose—one all people share—is to search for ways to reduce the danger of nuclear war . . . I believe we can do it."

March 23, 1983

Ronald Reagan speaks at the closing ceremony of the
United States–Soviet Union summit in Geneva on
November 21, 1985. Soviet leader Mikhail Gorbachev
insisted that SDI be discarded. Reagan responded by
assuring that SDI did not mean the United States would
launch a first strike against the Soviet Union. Although
the summit ended with this disagreement, the two
leaders pledged an arms reduction and agreed that a
nuclear war cannot be fought because it cannot be won.

others argued that it was too expensive and would not work. They said it would anger the Soviets and take the arms race into space.

The critics were right on most counts. SDI was very expensive. The research program cost about $4 billion a year. But from Reagan's point of view, nothing was more important to spend money on than national defense. The critics were right in saying it would not work, at least not with the technology that was available in the 1980s. Reagan did not expect it to be operational yet. He wanted to get the research started so scientists could figure out ways to make it work.

And critics were certainly correct in predicting that Reagan's proposal would anger the Soviet Union. Four days after Reagan's surprise speech, Yuri Andropov (1914–1984), who had replaced Brezhnev, called SDI "irresponsible" and "insane." He said the initiative was "putting the entire world in jeopardy." He predicted it would "open the floodgates of a runaway race of all types of strategic arms, both offensive and defensive."

THE RESULTS

SDI did restart the stalled arms race. After much debate, Congress approved funding for SDI and research started in 1984. The army, navy, and air force all began working on missile defense. Government laboratories made it their top priority. Private companies tried to come up with defensive weapons and systems. The secretary of defense created the Strategic Defense Initiative Organization (SDIO) to oversee all the separate projects.

During Reagan's presidency, SDI was nothing more than a research program. Scientists came up with designs for three types of new weapons—using lasers, particle beams, and rocket-powered interceptors. They determined that these weapons would be most effective against an ICBM during its boost, or first, stage. Since the boost stage lasts no more than five minutes, the defensive weapons would need to be positioned so they could respond in seconds. The researchers wanted to place them in satellite battle stations that would orbit the globe.

But none of these weapons or space stations were actually built. For a defense system to work, it has to be big enough to stop every single

Revelers topple the statue of KGB founder, "Iron Felix" Dzherzhinsky, in August 1991, after leaders associated with the KGB, or Russia's secret police, attempted a coup to undermine Mikhail Gorbachev's power. The failed coup marked the official end of Communism in Russia and the end of the Cold War. Celebrators draped Russia's white, blue, and red flag in front of the police agency as a commemoration to all the citizens the KGB sent to prison camps.

missile. But missiles could be manufactured much faster and far more cheaply than the weapons to shoot them down. While the United States built one satellite station for defense, the Soviets could be making hundreds of ballistic missiles for offense. Besides, an enemy could launch scores of decoys along with its real missiles, and the space lasers could be kept busy fighting the fake weapons.

But because there was always the hope of a breakthrough, the research continued. And the Soviet Union, ever afraid it would fall behind, raced to keep up. Soviet leader Andropov had pledged to match American development weapon for weapon. Both countries were spending millions on research for a system that neither would deploy. This battle to be best had an unexpected result. The economy of the United States was stronger than that of the Soviet Union, so the United States could afford the scientific research. The struggle to match Star Wars contributed to the Soviet Union's already failing economy. When the economy finally crumbled, the Communist government collapsed as well. In 1991, the Soviet Union dissolved as a giant nation, splitting up into several smaller countries. ■

A Patriot missile successfully intercepts a target in the sky above White Sands Missile Range in New Mexico. The solid rocket uses a ground-based radar to detect, identify, and track targets that may only be 10 to 20 feet (3 to 6 m) long, traveling at the speed of sound. The most recently upgraded missile, the Patriot Advanced Capability-3 (PAC-3), costs between $2 million and $3 million each.

4

SONS OF STAR WARS

The breakup of the Soviet Union radically changed the discussion about missile defense. None of the new countries to emerge from the ashes of the Soviet empire were superpowers. None appeared to have the desire or the ability to launch a massive assault against the United States. Was a missile defense still necessary?

Many argued that it was not. They pushed for an end to the expensive Star Wars program. Others pointed out that countries other than the former Soviet states had or

During the Six-Day War that Israel fought against Egypt, Jordan, and Syria in 1967, the Israeli offensive successfully seized the Sinai Peninsula, the West Bank, and the Gaza Strip. This Egyptian missile site in the Sinai Desert was equipped with Soviet ground-to-air missiles. The Soviet Union sold many arms to its Arab clients during the Cold War.

were developing nuclear weapons that could reach the United States. China had successfully tested a nuclear warhead as early as 1967. At least seven nations had obtained Scud ballistic (short-range, surface-to-surface) missiles from the Soviet Union during the Cold War: Afghanistan, Egypt, Iraq, Libya, North Korea, Syria, and Yemen. These countries had no nuclear weapons at the time, nor were they close to obtaining them. These Scud missiles could not have reached the United States. However, they could have reached an important strategic ally of the United States, Israel. Israel has always been concerned with defense because of tensions with some of these nations and their allies. However, some Americans worried that one day one nation might be able to hit America with even a small nuclear weapon, and that so much testing by so many countries with so little experience could accidentally release a missile.

GPALS

To protect against the new threat, President George H. W. Bush, who followed Reagan, decided to keep working on a missile defense program, but to scale it back. Because the program used some of the same types of space-based weaponry, people sometimes referred to it as Son of Star Wars. Instead of a thick shield that could protect the entire country, Bush focused on a thin shield that would defend against a small attack of up to 200 missiles. He called it Global Protection Against Limited Strikes (GPALS).

The centerpiece of GPALS was a technology developed under SDI. Edward Teller and others at Lawrence Livermore Labs had designed a weapons system they called "brilliant pebbles." It was to consist of thousands of small interceptors that would be placed in orbit and launched from space. Each pebble would have its own sensor and flight-control mechanism, so it could find and reach its target without the need for radar or a command station. However, the pebbles were designed so they would only activate upon human command. The pebbles were not ballistic and did not have warheads. They were to operate on kinetic energy, which means that they were to destroy their target simply by the force of their motion— they would knock into a missile at such incredibly high speed that the missile would break in pieces. Such a kinetic energy device is called a hit-to-kill weapon.

Bush did not depend solely on the space-based pebbles. He also developed ground-based weapons. One of the missiles was actually deployed in the Gulf War (1990–1991) against Iraq in 1991.

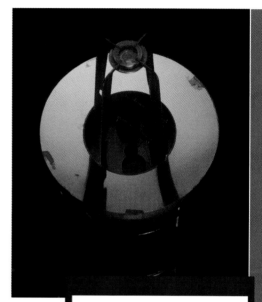

A brilliant pebbles weapons system consists of infrared detectors that sense the plumes of smoke exhausted from a ballistic missile's launch phase. If the target is determined to be hostile, the brilliant pebble will thrust, fire, and kill the target by colliding into it.

President George H. W. Bush is pictured here with Mikhail Gorbachev at a summit in Washington, D.C., on May 31, 1990. Bush supported Gorbachev in his efforts to reform the Communist nation, promising the Soviet leader that the United States would not seek to exploit the new nations that were once a part of the Soviet bloc for any political gain. One of the major accomplishments of Bush's term was START, the treaty that ended the weapons buildup between the two Cold War rivals.

Originally built as an antiaircraft weapon, the Patriot system was modified to shoot down short-range Scud missiles. Because the Patriot was a theater defensive weapon (used for war), not a strategic defensive weapon, it was not forbidden under the ABM Treaty. It did not perform as well as its inventors hoped. A government report found that it was successful in only 9 percent of its tries. An independent report said the Patriot destroyed probably one or two of the seventy or so Scuds Iraq launched.

THE THREAT FROM ROGUE STATES

Before long, the Gulf War faded into memory. George Bush was replaced by Bill Clinton (1946–) as president. Clinton's secretary of defense, Les Aspin, pronounced the "end of the Star Wars era." He shifted emphasis from strategic weapons to theater weapons, from national defense to battlefield defense. The Strategic Defense Initiative Organization became the Ballistic Missile Defense Organization (BMDO). Eighty percent of its funds went to developing weapons that would function in war. And the overall funds for all military projects were drastically cut. Very little was spent on national defense.

The need for a defense system became more critical in 1998. In that year, North Korea stunned the United States by testing an ICBM that could possibly reach the United States. Iran tested a missile that could strike anywhere in the nation of Israel. Clinton had thought both countries were at least five years away from such developments. And India and Pakistan shocked the world with tests of nuclear weapons. Suddenly a new threat became very real: an attack from a rogue state.

"Rogue state" is a phrase coined by the U.S. government for a country that does not abide by the standards of international behavior on which most civilized nations agree. Leaders of rogue states mistreat their own people, use their country's wealth for themselves instead of their citizens, lie, and break agreements they make. Sometimes they are aggressive toward their neighbors, and they often sponsor world terrorism. Rogue states are ruled very strictly and they are hostile to democratic countries. Their leaders often try to obtain weapons of mass destruction, including nuclear missiles. Because a rogue state does not follow international norms, no one is certain what it might do.

49

The Patriot missile is launched from anti-missile batteries after a radar detects the enemy's missile. The photo above shows the testing of such a launch. Used extensively in the first Gulf War, the battery failed to detect an incoming Iraqi Scud missile that succeeded in striking a U.S. army barracks, killing twenty-eight soldiers. More problems discovered since then include the missile's automatic response to incoming objects, which resulted in bringing down a friendly aircraft, a British fighter jet, in the war with Iraq in 2003.

New nuclear threats brought about new concerns and the revisiting of treaties created during the Cold War. Here, U.S. president Bill Clinton and Russian president Vladimir Putin meet in Moscow in 2000 to discuss the 1972 ABM Treaty. The United States' desire for a missile shield to protect against the threat of rogue states was in violation of the cornerstone treaty. The two leaders vowed at the meeting to make the ABM Treaty more effective in the age of new threats.

With the threat from rogue states becoming more and more worrisome, Republicans in Congress pressed Democratic President Clinton to do more about national missile defense. After much debate, President Clinton signed the National Missile Defense Act in 1999, almost a year after North Korea tested its ICBM. The legislation authorized the BMDO to resume research on developing a national missile defense system. The decision about whether to actually deploy the system would rest with the president. Clinton said he would make that decision in 2000.

ABM TREATY PROBLEMS

Researching and developing a missile defense system was one thing; deploying it was another. The biggest concern in deployment was the

1972 ABM Treaty. The agreement had been made between the United States and the Soviet Union. Even though the Soviet Union no longer existed, the treaty was still binding because Russia was the Soviet state that had signed it. The treaty allowed development of ABMs that were not ballistic, but permission to deploy them was up to a commission. So the United States might devise a great national missile defense system and not ever be allowed to use it. Clinton, however, assured the Russians that he had did not intend to back out of the ABM Treaty.

When the time came in 2000 to make the decision on deployment, Clinton could not say go. The system had failed two out of three tests. And the Russians insisted that deployment of the American system would violate the ABM Treaty. Clinton left the decision up to the next president.

The next president, George W. Bush (1946–), wanted strong missile defense. Like Reagan, he increased spending for the military, adding $5 million for missile defense in his first budget, bringing the total to $9 billion. He did not want to merely develop a system; he wanted to be able to deploy it. That meant he could not be bound by the thirty-year-old ABM Treaty. It was a deal struck in another era, against a different enemy, for outdated weapons. On December 13, 2001, President Bush announced that the United States would withdraw from the treaty, giving the six-month notice required. He explained that "the ABM treaty hinders our government's ability to develop ways to protect our people from future terrorist or rogue state missile attacks."

TWENTY-FIRST CENTURY NATIONAL MISSILE DEFENSE SYSTEM

Without the hindrance of the ABM Treaty, Bush pushed ahead with development of a limited defense system. His plan called for a fixed, land-based, non-nuclear system. Two sites were designated to protect against long-range ICBMs, one in Alaska and one in California. The Bush national missile defense system has five parts: two types of radar, an infrared system, a command system, and interceptors.

The first step in defense against an attack is to know that a strike is under way. The Upgraded Early Warning Radar detects an enemy missile

President George W. Bush announces the United States' withdrawal from the ABM Treaty, joined by the chairman of the Joint Chiefs of Staff General Richard Myers *(left)* and Secretary of State Colin Powell *(center)* on December 13, 2001. "Defending the American people is my highest priority as commander in chief and I cannot and will not allow the United States to remain in a treaty that prevents us from developing effective defenses," President Bush said.

in its midcourse phase, after a rocket has boosted it above Earth's atmosphere. This first radar alerts the X-band radar that a missile is on its way. The X-band radar tracks the missile as it comes closer. It can tell the difference between a warhead and a decoy. The infrared system, which is still being developed, is something like radar on a satellite. Instead of radar, it uses sensors to identify and follow ICBMs. It can detect a missile earlier than radar can. The plan calls for a set of twenty-four satellites to begin tracking hostile missiles from the moment they are launched.

All this information is relayed to the command system, the "brains" of the operation. The information is programmed into the interceptors and decisions are made about whether to launch the interceptors and how many to release.

The interceptor is the weapon. It is a kinetic, hit-to-kill missile that rams into an incoming ballistic missile. It has its own sensor that

COMMERCIAL SPIN-OFFS FROM MISSILE DEFENSE

Scientists who figure out how to build better missile defenses often discover and invent things that are useful in areas other than weaponry. Missile defense technology appears in hundreds of products that are used in everyday life. One is the airbag found in cars. Others are devices that purify water and machines that preserve food. Because of work on missile defense, doctors can perform T-PRK, a type of laser eye surgery. The research has produced better ways of sterilizing medical instruments. One company developed plastics that are resistant to air and moisture. It put the super-plastics to commercial use in beverage bottles and circuit boards. It also made them into medical tubing that allows doctors to insert miniature cameras and instruments into the human body to perform surgery through tiny incisions. Between 1984 and 1999, missile defense research created 338 commercial products.

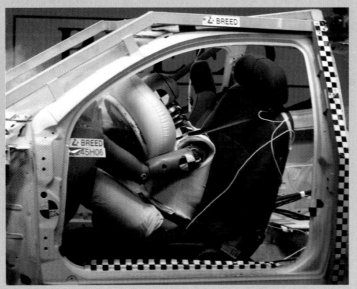

An airbag deploys for a crash-test dummy. The car-safety technology came out of missile defense research. When a detector senses a collision force, it signals the bag to inflate. This inflation force is equivalent to a solid rocket booster.

Included in the National Missile Defense (NMD) Act is the Ground Based Radar–X-Band Radar (XBR) that is pictured here *(and far right)*, located at the Ronald Reagan Ballistic Missile Defense Test Site in the Marshall Islands in the South Pacific. The XBR is the primary firing sensor, providing surveillance, tracking, discrimination, and interceptor support. NMD, a ground-based plan that focuses on limited missile attacks, is considered a toned-down version of the Strategic Defense Initiative.

enables it to home in on its target. If all goes well, it collides with the missile 120 miles (193 km) above Earth.

No one knows if all will go well. Scientists can test and soldiers can practice, but until the system is actually used, no one can tell whether it will work. Hitting a bullet with a bullet in midair takes very complex coordination. It requires split-second decision-making. It is astronomically expensive. And under the stress of a real-life threat, it might not even be possible. But the alternative is mass destruction.

It remains to be seen how effective the latest missile defense systems will be. The best we can hope for is that we will never have to find out. ■

[GLOSSARY]

ballistics The science that deals with motion effects and behavior of projectiles such as missiles when moving through the air.

boost phase First phase of a ballistic missile's path, during which the missile rises in the atmosphere with the rocket, or booster, still burning.

deploy Set in position ready for battle.

GPALS Global Protection Against Limited Strikes, name of the national missile defense research program under George H. W. Bush, which was aimed at protection against a small attack.

interceptor A ballistic missile or other device whose purpose is to strike and disable an offensive weapon while the offensive weapon is in flight.

kinetic Producing or depending on motion. A kinetic energy weapon depends on the force of its motion to destroy its target.

midcourse phase Middle portion of a ballistic missile's flight, during which the missile reaches its highest point and arcs back to Earth.

offensive weapons Weapons used for attack rather than defending.

payload The part of a missile that is meant to be delivered; the warhead.

strategic Having to do with accomplishing the objectives, or general plan, of a nation either in war or peace.

Strategic Defense Initiative Organization (SDIO) The agency in charge of national missile defense from 1984 to 1993, when it was renamed the Ballistic Missile Defense Organization.

terminal phase Last phase of a ballistic missile's flight, after the missile reenters Earth's atmosphere.

theater missiles Missiles used in warfare. Places where battles are fought are called theaters.

FOR MORE INFORMATION

Federation of American Scientists
171 K Street NW, Suite 209
Washington, DC 20036
Web site: http://www.fas.org

WEB SITES

Due to the changing nature of Internet links, the Rosen Publishing Group, Inc., has developed an online list of Web sites related to the subject of this book. This site is updated regularly. Please use this link to access the list:

http://www.rosenlinks.com/lwmd/aswp

FOR FURTHER READING

Baker, David. *Peace in Space*. Vero Beach, FL: Rourke Enterprises, 1988.

Baker, Lawrence W. *Cold War: Almanac*. Farmington Hills, MI: Gale Group, 2003.

Bankston, John. *Edward Teller and the Development of the Hydrogen Bomb*. Bear, DE: Mitchell Lane, 2002.

Fitzgerald, Frances. *Way Out There in the Blue: Reagan, Star Wars, and the End of the Cold War*. New York: Simon and Schuster, 2000.

Harshfield, James B. *Rock Street Five: The Mystery of the Computer Disks*. Lincoln, NE: iUniverse, 2000.

Olmos, David. *National Defense Spending*. Danbury, CT: Franklin Watts, 1984.

Pitt, Matthew. *Tomahawk Cruise Missile*. New York: Scholastic, 2000.

[BIBLIOGRAPHY]

Chandler, Robert W. *The New Face of War: Weapons of Mass Destruction and the Revitalization of America's Transoceanic Military Strategy*. McLean, VA: Amcoda Press, 1998.

Costanzo, Charles E. "Shades of Sentinel? National Missile Defense, Then and Now," *Air and Space Power Chronicles*, March 16, 2001 [online version] Retrieved June 18, 2004 (http://www.airpower.maxwell.af.mil/airchronicles/cc/costanzo.html).

Federation of American Scientists Web site. "National Missile Defense." Retrieved June 18, 2004 (http://www.fas.org/spp/starwars/program/nmd/index.html).

Graham, Bradley. *Hit to Kill: The New Battle Over Shielding America from Missile Attack*. New York: Public Affairs, 2001.

Missile Defense Agency Web site. "Ballistic Missile Defense Basics." Retrieved June 18, 2004 (http:// www.acq.osd.mil/bmdo/bmdolink/html/faq.html).

Union of Concerned Scientists Web site. "Global Security." Retrieved June 18, 2004 (http://ucsusa.org/global_security/missile_defense).

United States Navy, "Tomahawk Cruise Missile," Fact File, August 11, 2003. Retrieved June 18, 2004 (http://www.chinfo.navy.mil/navpalib/factfile/missiles/wep-toma.html).

[INDEX]

ABOUT THE AUTHOR

As a teacher, writer, and editor, Ann Byers is a lifelong learner. She continues to learn from her four grown children and their families. With her husband of thirty-three years, she divides her time between Fresno, California, and the San Francisco Bay area.